MENDING AND REPAIR OF BOOKS

MENDING AND REPAIR OF BOOKS

BY

MARGARET WRIGHT BROWN

KALPAZ

ISBN: 978-93-5128-718-6(PB)

First Published in 1916
Indian Reprint in 2017

Published by

Kalpaz Publications
C-30, Satyawati Nagar,
Delhi – 110052
E-mail: kalpaz@hotmail.com
Website: kalpazpublications.com
Ph.: +91-9212142040

CONTENTS

INTRODUCTORY NOTE

The task of mending demands so much of the time and energy of library workers and is a factor of such economic importance in every public library that it can not be put aside as incidental.

It is hoped that these suggestions may give definite aid in this homely task which is ever present in all libraries.

No attempt has been made to give instruction in the advanced processes of mending, as this at once encroaches on the art of binding.

The best mending can be done only where an acquaintance with the construction of the book has been acquired through a study of the various processes of binding. Librarians are urged to visit binderies to see the various processes and to study the art of binding under personal instruction of experienced binders whenever this is feasible.

It is not probable that any one librarian will use all of the processes suggested, and some of these will apply only to exceptional cases; but the directions cover diversified conditions in order that the librarian may have the necessary information whenever required.

The experienced mender. This handbook has not been prepared for the use of the larger libraries where a bindery is a part of the equipment, or where there are on the staff those trained in binding and hence experienced menders.

The inexperienced mender. The purposes of this handbook is to give practical aid and guidance to librarians who are entirely inexperienced in the work of mending and repair of books and whose knowledge must be gained through self-instruction.

The compiler has drawn upon many sources and has endeavored to make available the methods used in various operation and helpful suggestions received from librarians and practical binders.

Gratoful acknowledgment is herewith made for the cooperation and helpful suggestions received from various librarians and practical binders.

Iowa Library Commission,

Des Moines, Iowa.

MENDING AND REPAIR OF BOOKS

When to Bind or When to Mend

The question when to bind or when to mend is of daily recurrence, and a decision must be made upon the examination of every circulating book returned, before placing it on the shelves. The answer will depend largely on the policy of the library regarding the binding question.

No library can afford to circulate shabby, soiled or ragged books, because:

> (1) From an economic standpoint, a book's ultimate usefulness, or life, is materially shortened by neglect to bind at first sign of need.
>
> (2) When books are given proper care by the library, standards are set which insure a like treatment on the part of the reading public.
>
> (3) The reading public has a right to expect that its books shall be clean and whole, and that its property shall be in proper condition for satisfactory use.

To Bind

When the stitching breaks and a section or a few leaves are falling out, or about to fall out, the books should be sent at once to the bindery.

> This is happening daily with the original publishers' bindings. If the book is removed from the shelves the librarian is at once confronted by the problem of being unable to answer the unceasing cry for the last new novel, as it is the fiction which is usually in this condition. However, if the book is allowed to circulate a few more times there are "pages missing" and the book has become valueless.

No book should be rebound with pages missing.

When the stitches are not broken, but either a few or all the sections have become loose:

> There is no excuse for the librarian to leave upon her shelves or permit to circulate, books that are held together only by the slender threads with which they are sewed and threatening at any momont to come tumbling forth from the cover. Such books speak in no uncertain terms for rebinding or permanent withdrawal from the shelves.

Shall books be sent to the bindery when in the greatest demand?

YES, when they cannot be circulated further without permanent injury to them.

> Such books should be hastened through the bindery by statement to binder regarding immediate need. If your present binder cannot bind promptly, find one who will. A month is a reasonable time.
>
> The prompt rebinding of a book more than doubles its life. If the books have been reinforced at first sign of giving way (see page 16) all the temporary assistance which can safely be given has been rendered and if the book is of permanent value to the library it must be rebound.

To Mend

If the stitching has not broken.
If the joints are loose.
If the book has once been rebound.

The tendency among librarians is to mend too much before rebinding. Mending makes rebinding more difficult and jeopardizes the life of the book.

It is only in rare cases, such as the fact that a book is out of print, and yet valuable to the library, that a second rebinding is justified.

To Replace

Will it be cheaper to mend a book and, when its short life is done, withdraw and replace with a new copy?

YES, if the original cost is less than rebinding.

NOTE.—In the decision to replace, the labor of accessioning and withdrawal must always be taken into account.

The fresh, clean copies of the "easy books" and other good, inexpensive juvenile books, are to be preferred to rebound copies. If the original binding is so poor that a second copy would shortly be in the same condition as the first, it is then advisable to send the book promptly to the bindery for recasing. This insures double durability, and if the book has an attractive original cover it is preserved and the value of the book enhanced thereby.

YES, if the paper is of such spongy quality that the leaves break away from the stitching, and the book becomes shabby while the cover remains good. It does not pay to rebind.

YES, if the book is extremely soiled; replace, even if it costs more than rebinding.

YES, if a new edition, or better books on the same subject have been issued.

In replacing fiction, inexpensive editions are available for many popular titles in the Grosset & Dunlap edition, Burt Home Library, Everyman's Library, etc.

If inexpensive editions are used to replace, withdraw when worn out, and replace again with new copies. The paper is usually so poor that the folds will not hold the threads, and it does not pay to rebind.

SPECIAL LIBRARY BINDINGS

Several publishers have issued a few titles of fiction and juvenile books in a special library binding reinforced according to the specifications of the A. L. A. Committee on Binding.

These cost about 10c a copy more than the regular edition, but in many cases never need to be rebound, and a large part of the cost of binding is therefore saved. In every case the increased cost is amply repaid in increased service.

The publishers give ample notice of new titles that are to be published in this way, and they are also noted in the A. L. A. Booklist.

The number of old titles which are obtainable is small, and no complete list can be given since the publishers do not always keep a supply in stock. When ordering books, it is desirable to give general instructions that the special library binding is desired whenever available. Scribner and Houghton make a practice of issuing new titles of fiction and juvenile books in this binding.

THE MENDING TABLE: ITS SUPPLIES

A large piece of glass, cut either to fit the size of the table, or to cover a considerable portion, will be found most conducive to cleanliness, as it can be quickly and easily washed.

Paste. Library and Drawing Board paste, manufactured by Chas. M. Higgins & Co., Brooklyn, N. Y.

Local stationer can obtain prices, or order direct.

Library paste, dry (powder) form, mixed as needed.

Make according to recipe given on page 11.

Cloth. White outing flannel, cheese cloth and cheap grade of canton flannel, purchased by the yard at any dry goods store.

Art Vellum in assorted colors, cut in strips.

Cambric cut in strips.

Paper. Bond paper and onion skin, cut in strips; tissue paper.

Scissors. Slender, six-inch blade, good quality.

Knife. Shoemaker's long blade, square at end, or common paring-knife purchased at hardware store.

Folder. Bone, 15c, purchased at stationer's.

Needles. Darning.

Thread. Hayes' linen, No. 25; Barbour's linen, No. 40.

Pressing tins. 6x8 in. obtained at tin shop.

Cleansers. Wash for pages; wash for book covers; powdered pumice stone; art gum, 10c per cube, Sweet, Wallach & Co., Chicago, or from binder's supply house.

Shellac. Consult local druggist or paint dealer regarding the best white shellac.

Press. An old letter-press can usually be found in the community which may be purchased for a small sum. Prices on new copying press 10x12 in. may be obtained of local stationer.

Frequently a local bindery will suppy necessary mending materials. They can be obtained of any binder's supply house. A Librarian's Repairing Kit, fitted with necessary mending materials, may be purchased for $2.50 express prepaid. Information regarding this may be obtained of the State Library Commissions. Price list and samples of materials may be obtained from the following:

Democrat Printing Co., Madison, Wisconsin.
Gaylord Bros., Syracuse, New York.
Waldorf Bindery Co., Saint Paul, Minnesota.

PASTE, THE MENDING MEDIUM

Paste may be used with less danger of injury to the book than glue, and is the only mending medium which should be used on books that are to be rebound. ''Higgins' library and drawing board paste,'' not ''Higgins' photo paste,'' is very satisfactory for mending. It can be purchased in large jars and lasts a long time with care, and is cheaper than to make.

Use. Paste can be spread more evenly with the finger, and there is less waste than with a brush. Spread thinly, using only enough paste to make paper stick securely.

If a brush is desired, a soft paint brush one-half inch wide may be purchased at any drug store. The bristle brushes which come with the paste are not satisfactory.

A thick paste like the Higgins' spreads smoothly and is not taken up quickly by the paper. This is important, for if the paper stretches or expands the work can not be done in a satisfactory way.

Provide cheese cloth cut in small pieces for use in rubbing down the pasted parts, for keeping the fingers clean, etc. These should be used only a few times.

Cleanliness and neatness are absolutely essential to good mending.

Care. The Higgins' paste dries quickly and must have proper care. When the work is done push down with the finger all the paste which adheres to the sides of the jar. Make it even and smooth, covering this with two or three drops of water and screw the lid on tight.

Some librarians have found that a half a teaspoonful of formaldehyde added to a pint of library paste will keep it from spoiling for an indefinite period.

RECIPE FOR FLOUR PASTE

Wheat flour, 8 oz.
Powdered alum, ¼ oz.
Glycerine, 1½ oz.
Oil wintergreen, 1 dram.
Water, 1½ pts..

Dissolve alum in water and mix with flour into smooth, thin paste; cook in double boiler until smooth and clear; take from fire and add glycerine and oil of wintergreen. This quantity will make about one quart. After standing a day a watery fluid may collect on the paste—do not throw this away, but stir into paste. Keep this paste covered.

MUCILAGE

Under no condition should mucilage be used on any book which is to be rebound. Some librarians persist in doing this and then expect the binder to do good work. This cannot be done when a book has been so treated.

GLUE

Glue is a difficult medium for mending books. It should never be used except in books that are not to be rebound and only by experienced menders. A flexible glue is being used by the Public Library of Cincinnati, and other libraries. Information regarding this may be found in *Public Libraries*, October, 1909.

WAYS TO MEND

Avoid too much mending.

Paper used for mending should be cut lengthwise with the grain of the paper.

Cloth should be cut the long way of the material.

PAGES

Torn through the printing may be mended in several ways:

(1) Use ungummed, transparent mending paper, cutting it the size and shape of the tear, and about one-half inch wide. Apply a thin coat of paste to the strip and fit it carefully over the tear, having first placed a strip of waste paper under the torn leaf to absorb extra paste.

(2) Rub a very little paste on the torn edges, place torn edges together, then take a rather large piece of ordinary tissue paper and rub it gently along the tear so that the tissue paper will adhere to the torn edges.

Put under press and when dry the superfluous tissue paper should be torn off, using care to pull always towards the tear and from both sides at the same time.

The delicate fibre of the tissue paper acts as an adhesive and it is almost impossible to discern the way in which the mending has been done.

Torn in the margin

Use thin, firm mending paper, preferably a tint to match paper of the book.

Cut a strip one-half inch wide corresponding to the size and shape of the tear, apply paste and trim even with the edge of the leaf, or turn mending paper over the edge of the leaf, one-half inch, and paste down for added strength.

When these processes are used, place books in press until thoroughly dry.

Do not use gummed paper for this work.

LEAVES

When loose leaves are replaced the greatest care should be taken to make sure that they do not extend beyond the edge of the book. If this occurs, it shows careless or inexperienced mending.

Loose leaves may be inserted in several ways:

1.

> If the leaf fits exactly into the book, it may be tipped in by applying paste to one-eighth inch of the inner margin.
>
> Place the loose leaf in the book, the outer edge even with the book, and rub down the pasted inner margin against the next leaf with bone folder.
>
> Put the book in press until dry.

Illustrations may be tipped-in in this way when it is desirable to preserve them.

2.

> If it is found by measuring that the leaf when inserted, will extend beyond the edge of the book, fold the leaf at the inner margin over a ruler edge, or other straight edge, slightly more than one-eighth of an inch, thus making a hinge. Apply paste to this hinge with the finger. Place leaf in the book and push well back; rub the little pasted hinge down with bone folder, being careful to leave no free paste.

3.

> In case the quality of the paper of the leaf to be inserted will not stand the tipping-in process, or is badly worn at the inner margin, it may be inserted by a guard. Fold a half-inch strip of bond, or onion skin paper, lengthwise. Apply a thin coat of paste to the outside of this strip. Bond paper stretches immediately upon application of moisture, and to avoid this as much as possible, the work should be done quickly. Onion skin does not stretch. Attach half of the strip to the inner edge of the loose leaf, and the other half to the adjoining page in the book, close in by the fold. Trim edge of leaf if it projects. Put in press until dry.

Do not use gummed muslin for this work. It destroys the chance of proper rebinding and detracts from the appearance of the rebound book.

SECTIONS

When more than one section, sometimes called signature, is loose in a book which is to be rebound, it should be rebound at once.

If the thread in one section only is broken, or if one section only is loose in a rebound book, or one not worth rebinding, and the rest of the binding is intact,—

Loose sections may be inserted as follows:

> **Loose-back books.** Open the book at the place where the section is loose. (When the book is open the back of the book separates from the cover.)
>
> Open the loose section and place it in the proper position in the book. Near the top and bottom in the center fold of the section will be seen the holes which were made by the binder.
>
> Thread a three-inch darning needle with Barbour's linen thread No. 40, or Hayes' linen thread No. 25.
>
> Pass the needle through the hole at the top of the loose section and out between the book and its loose back. Do not pull the thread clear through.
>
> Drop the needle and thread down between the back of the book and the loose back to the bottom.
>
> Run the needle and thread from the outside in through the hole at the bottom of the loose section.
>
> Pass the needle and thread around again in the same way. Draw tight and tie with a hard knot at the point of beginning.

If the folds of the leaves in the loose section are torn or thin, they should be mended before replacing the section. Take a half-inch strip of thin, firm paper, the length of the page; fold through the middle lengthwise and paste down through the center fold of the leaves.

Tight-back books. Not to be rebound.

Cut a guard of cambric, or bond paper, three-fourths of an inch wide and as long as the book; fold in the middle.

Sew the section to the middle of the guard.

Paste the guard in the book, attaching half of it to each of the leaves adjoining the loose section. Push well back in the book, and rub down well.

JOINTS

Books in the ordinary case or publishers' binding will, after a short period of use, show signs of weakness in the joints (where the book and cover are attached). The paper cracks and both it and the super on the back of the book loosen, and unless immediate attention is given the stitching breaks and the book must go to the bindery.

Super is a loosely woven cotton cloth which is glued on the back of books to help hold the sections together, and extends on to the inside of the cover to help hold the book and cover together. In the publishers' bindings, this super is usually all that holds a book in the cover.

Loose joints may be

Reinforced. Take a strip of firm paper or cambric to be used as a guard. Cut this strip the length of the book, fold down the middle and apply thick paste so that the paper will not stretch.

Paste one-half of this strip to the fly leaf and rub down. Lay blotting paper on this. Paste the other half of the strip on the cover of the book; apply paste between the loose back and the book; close the book and rub thoroughly the back of the book and the joint with a bone folder.

Care should be taken to push the book well back in the cover.

Recased

If the stitching has not broken, and the paper is of good quality, the book may be removed entirely from the cover and recased.

In recasing, the greatest care must be given and books must be in condition specified to obtain satisfactory results.

> Take a sharp knife and cut through the super on each side of the cover. This super is easily lifted from the book cover. Pull it off the back of the book, taking great care in this.
>
> Take white outing flannel, which is light in weight and double-faced, or canton flannel (downy side towards the book), or cheesecloth; cut a strip as long as the back of the book, and two inches wider; paste this over the back, allowing an inch extension on each side; rub down well with bone folder and let dry. Hold the back of the book so that the sections, or signatures, will not separate.
>
> Apply paste to the back of the book and to cover, place book in the cover, pushing well back.
>
> Paste down one inch extension of cloth on each side of cover, laying blotting paper between it and the book. Rub thoroughly with bone folder the back of the book and the joints.
>
> Make guard for joint, following instruction for reinforcing, and let dry before using. The book should then be carefully pressed open in the same way as a new book.

Picture books, or very thin books, where the stitching is not broken, but out of cover or sewing loose, may be recased by above method.

PRESSING

This adds greatly to the appearance of the mended or repaired books. Do not place weights over the rounded back of the book.

Place the pressing boards or tins over the book boards only, even with, but not extending over, the joint.

Pressure on the rounded back will weaken the book in the most vital part.

MISSING PAGES

If a page is missing and it is impossible to replace the book with a new copy, the page may be typewritten and tipped in.

When it is necessary to rebind the book, the margin of the typewritten page should be left an inch larger, all around, than the regular margin. This is for the convenience of the binder who will trim down the margin in process of rebinding.

Make typewritten page conform to size and shape of printed page.

NOTATION FOR DAMAGES

When there is an injury to a book which is allowed to remain in circulation, the reading public should be made aware that the damage is known to the library by a notation, with date, near the injury, e. g.,

"Damage noted 1 Mr. '10, Free Public Library."

WAYS TO CLEAN

The book should be cleaned as well as mended. Too much attention cannot be given to the cleanliness of the books in circulation.

There is nothing that more quickly creates a distaste for the use of a public library than the handling of one soiled and grimy book.

PAGES

A good, soft sponge rubber, which is much better than an ordinary eraser; bread that is not perfectly fresh, and which can be rolled in a ball; or powdered pumice stone, rubbed on with a piece of clean cloth, may be used for cleaning soiled pages in the following way:

> Rub gently and slowly, and hold the page flat with the left hand to prevent tearing.
>
> Rub from inner margin of the page outward, to prevent crumpling.
>
> Brush off carefully all particles of bread or rubber, or pumice stone, allowing none to remain in the folds between the leaves.

Mud stains may be removed by using a soft brush or sponge, with a preparation of the following proportions: One cup water, one teaspoon ammonia, four drops carbolic acid.

Avoid too much rubbing or print will blur.

Slip the pressing tin under the page, and after washing, place white blotting paper on each side of the leaf.

Ink stains may be removed by one of the standard ink eradicators to be obtained of local stationer or druggist.

COVERS

Soiled covers may be cleaned by using rubber, pumice stone, soap and water. The best results are obtained by the use of the following wash:

> Two parts good vinegar and one part water. Apply with a clean cloth and rub hard until dirt is removed, then place upright to dry. This should not be used on leather.
>
> the book should then be shellacked.

Shellacked covers. New books may receive preliminary care by shellacking before placing in circulation. Shellacking the covers, especially those in light colors, provides great protection from dirt, and they are then easily washed with the vinegar and water. Another coat of shellac is advisable after washing.

> To shellac, hold the book by the printed matter and apply the shellac, which may be diluted with a little wood alcohol, taking care to shellac the edges well. Give two coats; between coats, suspend on a cord over night to dry. After the last coat, rub with soft cloth slightly oiled with clock or olive oil. This prevents sticking.
>
> If the books are labeled before shellacking, the ink must be allowed to dry thoroughly or it may run; in removing the labels, use wood alcohol first to cut the shellac, and then soak with blotting paper and water.

Care should be taken in the selection of the shellac; if not, the books will be gummy and hard.

To prevent the cracking and splitting of the leather in bound magazines, place a few drops of olive oil in small squares of sheet wadding, gather up the corners and rub over the leather; wipe off surplus oil with a soft cloth. This may be done once or twice a year.

Worn covers may be replaced on books with leather backs by removing cloth from the boards dry, and using this as a pattern from which to cut new cloth or paper. Re-line inside of boards with paper.

Covers split at joint. Strips of cloth in assorted colors may be obtained with other mending supplies to reinforce covers split at the joints.

This cloth may be obtained gummed or ungummed; if ungummed, use glue; if gummed, moisten with thin paste.

BINDING RECORD

Preparation of books for the bindery. Closely associated with the work of mending and repair of books is that of the preparation of books for the bindery. Binders have complained of the careless and unbusiness-like methods of some librarians in this matter. Attention should always be given to the following:

> Handle a book to be bound with more care than when the binding is sound.
>
> Collate every book to make sure that no pages are missing, unless it is ascertained that the binder includes this process in his work.
>
> Make a binding slip for each book. Write plainly on the slip the lettering which is to be placed in each panel on the back of the book.
>
> This supplies copy for the "finisher" to follow. It is frequently necessary in rebinding to reduce the lettering in the title, and the librarian should decide how the title is to read.
>
> Some binders will letter name of the library in bottom panel without extra charge, if the library will have a die made.

Binding slips can be purchased from the Library Bureau or Democrat Printing Company for so little that it is advisable to purchase rather than to take the time to make. Some binders will supply these without charge.

Magazines should be carefully examined to make sure that each volume is complete, including title page and index. The librarian should write to the publisher for these, if they are not received within a reasonable time after the volume is completed. If missing, instruct binder to bind in stubs so that they may be inserted when obtained.

Send an alphabetical list with the books to the bindery for checking purposes. Keep a duplicate copy.

File alphabetically in charging tray the book cards which have been removed from the books; charge these to the bindery.

When books are returned from the bindery. Examine carefully for flexibility (books should open flat); evenness of cover; compactness; correct and even lettering; reasonably wide margins.

Check books with duplicate list.

Pay no bills until all mistakes are rectified. Mistakes in lettering can be corrected, and when this occurs return to the bindery.

Enter in accession book under "remarks," opposite the entry of each book the date when the book was rebound: e. g., "reb'd 1 D 09"; also on inside of lower front cover near the joint. A rubber stamp at small expense may be ordered from any stamp works, with the word "reb'd" to be inserted in the pencil date holder with the date. This saves writing.

Enter on the monthly report blank the total number of books rebound. (This gives data for yearly total and obviates the necessity of keeping binding book.)

TEMPORARY BINDERS

The Gaylord Bros.' pamphlet binder provides an inexpensive magazine binder, both for the current periodicals in use in the reading room and those in circulation. The cover of the magazine may be pasted on the outside of the binder, and after the current month the magazine may be circulated just as a book, without damage for future binding.

SCRAP BOOKS

When the illustrated juvenile books have fallen apart or must be withdrawn, very attractive scrap books may be made by cutting out the pictures and pasting them in scrap books, which can be procured in various sizes from the Democrat Printing Co., Madison, Wis., the Waldorf Bindery Co., St. Paul, Minn., and other binderies.

Information as to terms used in binding and mending and illustrations of the structure of a book may be found in the following:

Cockrell, Douglass—Book binding and the care of books ....Appleton $1.25

Dana, J. C.—Book binding for libraries ....Library Bureau .75

MENDING AND REPAIR OF BOOKS

—MARGARET WRIGHT BROWN

This handbook offers a manual to mending and repairing of books. It describes in detail when to bind and when to mend a damaged book, how to mix and use paste to mend a book, the supplies you will need to mend and repair books, how to repair torn pages, how to mend loose covers, and what do to about missing pages in a damaged book. Originally published in 1921,it aims to teach the librarians book repair techniques that were current at the time.Though the methods described in the book have likely been improved upon since this book was originally published, the book remains a valuable resource for those who are interested in learning about the history of library science, or in getting a sense for how librarians managed torn and otherwise damaged books in the early 1920s.

KALPAZ PUBLICATIONS

Treasuring Books on Humanities & Social Sciences

Delhi-110052 Ph.: 9212142040 E-mail: kalpaz@hotmail.com

Distributed by:

GYAN BOOKS PVT. LTD.

5, ANSARI ROAD, DARYA GANJ, NEW DELHI- 110002 (INDIA)

Mob.: 9811692060

E-mail: books@gyanbooks.com www.gyanbooks.com

Price: ₹ 100

ISBN: 978-93-5128-718-6

9 789351 287186